'Talk

The art of speaking
Wenglish

By

John Edwards

2003

TIDYPRINT PUBLICATIONS

CREIGIAU

Dedication

To Mair, my wife, with gratitude
for all her help and encouragement.

This new edition first published by
Tidyprint Publications, 2003

First published by D. Brown & Sons Ltd, 1985

This edition printed by
Chas Hunt & Company (Cardiff) Ltd

Distributed by Welsh Books Council
Unit 16, Glanyrafon Enterprise Park, Llanbadarn, Aberystwyth, Ceredigion SY23 3AQ
Tel: 01970 624455
e-mail: www.cllc.org.uk

Illustrations by *Gren*

FOREWORD

Almost twenty years have elapsed since *Talk Tidy* was first published, so it is with some sense of disbelief that the reissued books are commended.

I am much indebted to Don Llewellyn and Brian Wood for their enthusiastic encouragement and involvement; and particularly to Brian, who has shown great skill, tenacity, and patience in ensuring success to the enterprise.

Sincere thanks to Gren; I count it a great privilege that this incomparable artist has decided to contribute.

John Edwards

December 2003

Introduction

The Welsh dragon with its forked tongue, it is often said, is able to speak two languages: Welsh, the ancient tongue of a Celtic people; which some confidently claim to be the very 'language of heaven', and English, which, by now, is the language of most Welsh men and women following its importation from across Offa's Dyke.

It is my confident assertion, however, that the dragon has not merely two tongues, but three. The third is 'Wenglish', the language of the South Wales valleys communities, where a unique blend of residual Welsh and the distinctive patterns of spoken English is to be heard. It is the authentic voice of Anglo-Welshness in large areas of Gwent, Mid and West Glamorgan, and needs to be seen as the oral 'badge of identity' for many who live in these areas and as a vital element in their social heritage.

Rhymney Valley author Richard Felstead, head of department in a comprehensive school in that valley and himself a product of a South Wales mining community, has described Wenglish memorably: "It is the prattle of the pit, the word-spinning of the Workmen's Club, the eloquence of the eisteddfod, the clatter of the chapel, the gossip over the garden-wall, the ranting on the rugby field, and the palaver of the playground. Wenglish remains, and will always be, the language of those capable of talking the hind-legs off a dragon." My own deep and abiding interest in Wenglish is the result of returning to live in my home-town Abercynon, after thirty years of 'exile' in Bristol and North Wales (two places with unmistakable language-patterns), and finding that the speech patterns and rhythms of my childhood and boyhood, so far from being dead and buried, are alive and flourishing. Wenglish, it seems to me, is eminently worthy of putting down on record as evidence of its survival and continuing existence.

Reactions to talks which I have given on Radio Wales and Radio Cymru, to organisations of many and varying kinds, in after-dinner speeches, and in 'poems-and-pints' sessions (or in more 'up-market', 'crachach' assemblies which merit the title 'vodka and verse' or 'sayings and songs'), have convinced me how real and alive is the interest of people throughout South Wales (and in places 'up England way' where exiles gather) in their 'very own language'.

The voice of the non-Welsh-speaking majority of South Walians is not always heard as often or as purposefully as it ought to be. With all the attention which, rightly, is given to the place of the Welsh language in Wales, it is not surprising that the monoglot native of South Wales suffers at regular intervals from some of the symptoms of 'identity crisis'. There is a distinctive, readily-recognised, and wholly authentic, indigenous speech which many non-Welsh-speaking local inhabitants excel at using. It is a form of speaking which retains the rhythms, refrains, cadences and inflections of Welsh, but one which shows, also, the major influence of the one-time alien language – English – which was brought to South Wales from many areas in Britain and elsewhere, when the onward march of the industrial revolution turned the region into a British 'Klondyke'.

1

So closely does Wenglish parallel and echo the sounds and rhythms of spoken Welsh that it is not surprising that it is often said by experts in linguistics (some of them products of this area): 'Of course they still speak Welsh in the valleys – but now, they speak it through the medium of English.' Sometimes, original Welsh words and expressions are retained for use in current Wenglish: the worst thing you can say about a local housewife is that she is 'didoreth'. 'Didoreth' is a good Welsh word, but the definition provided by the standard Welsh dictionary – 'feckless' – is grossly inadequate to convey all the impact and vitality that this word shows in its Wenglish usage. (See the glossary of words and terms.) Other examples of original Welsh words retained in Wenglish are 'twp/twpsin', 'clec', 'jawl', 'screch,' and 'crachach'.

There are Welsh words discernible in Wenglish which have been corrupted and mutated: 'gibbons' from 'sibwns' (spring onions), 'twti-down' (crouch or squat), 'shiggle' from 'siglo' (to shake), and 'wit-wat' from 'chwit-chwat' (fickle, changeable) offer some examples of this process.

There are Welsh expressions which have been translated more or less directly for use in Wenglish – 'there's nice to see you' from 'dyna braf I dy weld'; 'to raise the ashes' from 'codi'r lludw'; 'to rise a ticket' from 'codi tocyn', and perhaps the most unfortunate bequest from Welsh is seen in the double-negative form as in 'I haven't got none' from ' 'does dim gennyf'.

Another legacy from the syntax of the Welsh language clearly found in Wenglish is the emphatic form of statement which exactly reproduces the word-order of Welsh speech and writing. Fluent Wenglish speakers will often say, "No mun, Baptist I am, see!", or "Manager he was, not foreman!" or, "A pound I wanted, not three-quarters!" or, "Over by there it is!" or "Go you!". This echo of Welsh is also seen clearly in statements like, "You know, gul, in school with us she was!".

It is hoped that this book will enable people who are products of the Wenglish-speaking communities to identify with and to take some pride in a way of speaking which is theirs, and theirs alone, since the prime objective in compiling this book is to celebrate the very existence of Wenglish. Perhaps, like me, many local people shudder when they hear spurious, 'stage-Welsh' expressions like 'indeed to goodness look you now!' Shakespeare and his improbable characters like Fluellen who feature in the historical plays are to blame for this. Who knows, some local playwright may be encouraged to write a masterpiece about life as it really is 'round 'ere', containing authentic gems like, "Damn, aye mun. I do work days reg'lar - top pit."

To the purists and scholars of linguistics of the classical school, much of Wenglish is slovenly and unacceptable in a world where indivuality and regional identification are not always encouraged. Certainly, there are slovenly features in Wenglish and the most common example of slovenly speech, the 'I do' syndrome, which refers to the habit of many locals saying, 'I do 'ave, 'I do like' or (perhaps the worst of all) 'I do do', sounds unattractive to a delicate ear. Yet, it ought to be remembered that such speech forms were common in forms of English in days long ago.

2

There should be no doubt that there are elements in the everyday speech of Wenglishmen and Wenglishwomen which offer examples of warmth, colour, vitality, and texture in spoken language, features which Standard English by its very nature can never possess. In a shrinking world in which far-flung global travel is taken for granted, the need to speak Standard English is obvious. Without doubt, English is the number-one language for effective world-wide communications; the emergence of the USA as a world-power and the adoption of English as the language of international communication by the world's airlines have ensured this.

Wenglish then, is not for speaking to foreigners. It is obvious that foreigners in a geographical sense who make their presence felt from Calais onward will not understand our local speech. But there are also foreigners in the linguistic sense of the word – and they begin at Cardiff (Cairdiff), Brecon, Abergavenny and West Swansea – who will not readily understand Wenglish. It is hoped that this book will provide insight into local speech for those 'indigenous foreigners' and will enable them to understand what is being said when they hear 'a real mouthful of Wenglish'.

In setting down some of the words and expressions used by fluent speakers of Wenglish, the ambivalence shown by many of them in the use of the letter 'aitch' has been taken into account. Like their Celtic cousins in other West British areas, they show some confusion between the name of this letter and its sound, this is apparent in 'Haitch T.V.' or in the use of a popular relish called 'Haitch P. Sauce'. Because there are, in Wenglish, examples both of over-stressing the aspirate and totally disregarding it, it has been found necessary to show this in order to try to catch some, at least, of the true flavour of this speech form.

A glossary of words, phrases, and expressions is provided, usually with a 'translation' in Standard English. This, it is hoped, will encourage both the 'foreigner' and the dedicated learner. In the last section of the book some 'News in Wenglish' items, some traditional stories, and some Aesop's fables have been included. Because the traditional material is familiar and well-loved, it has not been thought necessary to provide a Standard English version, since all should find it possible to follow the story-line without undue difficulty. Words which belong to local speech and which were more commonly used when I was a child and a young man have been included, although some of them are seldom heard nowadays – at least, not in Abercynon; which for many years past has been a very much Anglicised area. They are included because they help to provide a clear guide to how local speech developed when many Welsh-speaking residents, having moved from other parts of Wales to the mining areas, were making the laborious and painful transition to speaking English which was already a dominant force in local speech. Abercynon came into existence first because of the canal (its first name was 'Navigation'); it developed with the advent of the Taff Vale Railway, changing its name to 'Aberdare Junction' and then, as the colliery became the prime source of work, its present name was adopted. Is it any wonder that English was the foremost influence in local speech? Yet, the influence of Welsh was also apparent. When lining up for the Workmen's Hall on Saturday mornings to see the latest Hollywood epic, we urged others not to 'cheat the gwt'. It would occasion some surprise to hear that word today, because the French word 'queue' (pronounced 'kew') has long since supplanted the Welsh word 'gwt'. It would produce equal surprise if I heard a local child who was given a 'cwlff' or 'cwlffyn' (a thick hunk of bread and butter – a 'doorstep'). The very-much-used word of childhood, 'swanky' seems long since to have gone, now replaced by the improbable but undeniably popular word, 'posh' (a derivative of 'port-out-starboard-home').

Wenglish is essentially a spoken language. This causes very real problems when attempts are made to write down some of the distinctive, often-spoken, rarely-written words in cold print. Like most local people I know that the word 'bosh' is the kitchen – sink and that it was originally an iron-works word from the days when they used to be so prominent a feature of the landscape of what is now called 'The Heads of the Valleys' area and in parts of Swansea and its hinterland and in the Neath area. I have used the word countless times, but I have yet to see it written down. Perhaps the word which can genuinely claim to be ours, and only ours, is the warmest and best-loved word, 'cwtch'. It used to convey a number of meanings and these are detailed in the glossary. Its warmest and most splendid meaning occurs in 'Cwtch up to youer (your) mam!'. It is only faintly insulting to Wenglishfolk to suggest that 'cuddle' or 'snuggle' have the same warmth as 'cwtch-up'. The only possible, adequate mental picture to conjure up the true eloquence of this word is that of a child who is being nursed 'Welsh-fashion'.

It may be of interest to note that one use of the word 'cwtch', fondly recalled from childhood, seems to have disappeared. This was the use made when, in droves, the local youngsters went out to pick blackberries and, having found a bush dripping with succulent fruit, would shout, 'Bar cwtch! bar cwtch!' ('Don't come near my cwtch!'), to warn off anyone who might attempt to share the treasure trove.

A Glossary of Wenglish words and phrases

It should not be assumed that all the words and expressions recorded here are unique to Wenglish-speaking areas; it is obvious that a number of English words are present. Many local people believe that the word 'moithered', for example, is Welsh. It is, of course, an English dialect word which is pronounced 'moidered' in Midlands areas like Staffordshire and 'mythered' in Lancashire and elsewhere in the North of England.

What is special is that, in the rhythms and cadences of Wenglish, a new and distinctive flavour is given to 'imported' words. Useful examples of this process are provided when one considers the way in which local people talk of their state of health when they 'don't feel up to the mark' or are 'under the weather'. Wenglish folk are seldom ill; they are sometimes 'bard' and are truly far from well when 'bard in bed' and 'under the doctor'.

The word 'piece' when used to mean a round of bread and butter provides another example of the way in which words are put to use, and 'piece' is a word which evokes a treasured memory of childhood – that of sitting around a table at meal-times. The

4

prepared 'mound' of bread and butter, often cut in 'cwlffs' or cwlffyns' had already disappeared with a rapidity which testifies to the keen appetites of 'growing boys and girls' – and still more was needed! In turn, we children would say, "Piece, please, Mam", and another helping of basic food was procured. What a fundamental part of childhood bread and butter was! There were very few items of food with which it was *not* essential to eat bread and butter. It was a childhood ambition of mine – shared by many others, surely – to be able to eat tinned fruit (tin fruete) without having to include its obligatory accompaniment!

It is the way in which words like 'moithered', 'bard', 'peaky', 'rough', etc., etc., are pronounced and strung together which, together with the emotional content in word-delivery, impart a unique flavour to Wenglish. This is due, in part at least, to the fact that we are such a splendid ethnic mix 'round 'ere, and it matters not whether your grandparents or great-grandparents came from Dowlais or Dublin, from Lampeter or Leominster, from Bangor or Birmingham, from Trawsfynydd or Timsbury – they all contributed to that marvellous mixture called South Walians. The Davieses and the Donovons, the Bevans and the Battrams, the Cadwalladers and the Colemans, the Howellses and the Hobbses met, courted, married, and inter-married, giving the 'ethnic brew' a pungency of flavour and filling the valleys with a lilting 'lingo' of a special kind which even the great exodus of the depression years could do little to diminish.

To claim that this is an exhaustive glossary, complete in every detail would be presumptious. There will certainly be those from this area and from other parts of South Wales who will say that I have omitted, forgotten, or never heard of words and expressions which they know. To them I offer sincere apologies and can only say in mitigation that 'I have racked my brains, hunted high and low, listened to heaps of people and have been at it "frages", doing my level best' to compile as comprehensive a list of Wenglish words, phrases, and expressions as one person can manage. Even so, I know I shall 'kick myself' when words are suggested which I know I should have included.

·

5

6

Glossary

A

Ach-a-fi: An expression of disgust, as in, "You should have seen the state the place was in – ach-a-fi!" (Welsh)

According: Depending, as in, "It's all according to the weather, innit?"

After: Later on; "Come up to my house after, will you?"

Afto: Wenglish for 'have to'.

Again/Agen: Later on; this causes 'foreigners' most problems when they hear, "Don't give it to me now, *give it to me again/agen.*" *It never means 'once more'. See 'now jest'.*

Against: A translation of the Welsh 'yn erbyn', meaning 'by the time' as in, "Against I'd washed the dishes, there was no time to clean the house."

Ages: Frages/issages: 'Frages' is Wenglish for 'for ages' and 'issages is the Wenglish equivalent of 'this ages'; "I haven't seen you frages", or "I haven't been to the pictures 'issages".

Aggravate: To annoy, as in, "Will you stop aggravating people with all your questions?"

Agony, in: Extreme pain; "I had toothache chronic – in agony for days, I was!"

Aim: To throw, as in, "Stop aiming stones, will you?"

All jaw: Idle, empty speech; "Pay no attention – he's all jaw, that one!"

All taken away: Refers to what is called 'woman's trouble'; "She've been let out of hospital now, but, poor dab, she've 'ad it all taken away …"

Alley/Alley bomper: A child's marble (game). The alley bomper is a small metal marble.

All right: Pronounced 'awright?'; one of the local greetings; see 'shw mae' and 'hi-ya'

All over you: Making a great fuss; "e's all over you one minute, then pretends 'e don't know you from Adam the next …"

All show/all swamk: All 'front-window dressing' with little or nothing to back up the image.

Alter; will he? Change his ways, as in, "There's times I do wonder will 'e ever alter?"

All there: An expression to show admiration for someone's ability, as in, "He's all there, that one – he knows his way about."

Always the same: Constant, unvarying; "She's always the same, comes on to talk every time she sees you …"

'Ambarg: Wenglish for 'handbag'.

Apartments: Pronounced 'partmunts'; to live in 'partmunts' is to have separate rooms sharing someone else's house; *not* to be confused with 'living through and through'.

Anch/Ansh: A bite, or taste, as in, "Give us an anch of your apple, will you?"

Apron: A pig's caul, used in making faggots

Article: Person, as in, "Funny article he is – never know what he'll be up to next".

As good as look at you: Without a qualm or second thought; "A real rogue, that one – he'll rob you right, left and centre as good as look at you!"

Ashman, the: Wenglish for the refuse collector.

Away: Not from these parts, as in, "I'm not from 'round 'ere – I'm from away,like."

Aye-aye: (1) The single 'aye' is Wenglish for 'yes'. The double form is often used as a as a reply to 'shw mae?', 'awright?', owbe?", or Hi-ya?'.
(2) Affirmative or most positive confirmation, as in, "Well aye-aye mun, he's right enough there, you know!"

B

Babi-lol: One wanting much attention, a 'big baby'

Bach/Fach: Not used to convey 'small' as a literal translation of the Welsh word would indicate. As in Welsh usage, 'Jim bach' or Mair fach' are used to mean 'dear Jim' or 'dear Mair'.

Back-back: Wenglish for 'reverse' as in advice to motorist "Back-back a bit, then you'll see the turning you're after …"

Back and fore: Wenglish for 'back and forth' as in, "He's a real pest – back and fore, back and fore, all the time!"

Back (out the): In the back garden or at the rear of the house. This expression lost much of its impact with the advent and increasing popularity of indoor toilets …

Bag of nerves/Bag a nerves: In a sorry state, as in, "Since that happened to her, she's nothing but a bag of nerves".

Bailey: Usually the back yard; "She do sweep 'er bailey reg'lar as clockwork …"

Bald-headed: In a reckless manner; " 'E don't stop to think – 'e goes at it bald-'eaded!"

Bar: Except, as in, "They were all there, bar one".

Bara-bit: Very small piece; "Only a dwt, she is – no bigger than a bara-bit!"

Bard: Wenglish for 'ill'; "I was bard, mun, I was in 'ospital frages."

Batch: A small round, flattish loaf of bread.

Bathers: Wenglish for 'swimming trunks' or 'bathing costume'.

Beanfeast: A fine meal, as in, "We had a real beanfeast after the wedding".

Belonging to: Related; "Of course he's belonging to you – his mother and your gran are first cousins."

Belter: A heavy blow or beating; "You're asking for a belter if you don't shut up!"

Beauties: Pronounced 'bewties', meaning excellent specimens; "Sorry, we're sold out of them, but we 'ad bewties last week!"

Beauty: Pronounced 'bewty'; a fine one in the derogatory sense; "You're asking a bewty in him – he's hopeless!"

Before: In preference to, as in, "Give me shopping in Ponty, before there, anytime!"

Beholden: Indebted; "I'm not asking for help, I won't be beholden to anyone, then"

Belfago: Loudly; "He was singing real belfago in the bath."

Bell (on every tooth): Used to describe someone who speaks often – and loudly, as in, "She's at it again, you can hear her a mile off – she's got a bell on every tooth!"

Bellyful: Enough – and more! "I'm giving it up. I've had a real bellyful of this now!"

Beyond: Extremely, as in, "That kid is cheeky beyond!"

Bigger liar than Tom Pepper: An outrageous teller of untruths.

Bit of: In a small way, as in, "He's a bit of a singer/plumber/decorator" or "They've got a bit of a car park behind the shop"

Bitter: Wenglish for 'bit of'; I gorrw keep it tidy, it's my bitter best, like …"

Black as the ace of spades: Very dirty.

Blacklead: Wenglish for 'pencil'

Bladder: Wenglish for 'balloon'

Blemmer/Brammer: Excellent, as in, "Them pears are real blemmers/brammers". The 'a' sound in 'brammers' is elongated to sound like 'braahmers'.)

Block: A log or firewood; "Let's have another block on the fire, it's a sharp one tonight".

Bloke/Bloak: Man, as in, "He's the bloke from the Prudential".

Boil tam: Wenglish for 'boiled ham'

Bomper: Big; "They've had twins – and one of them is a real bomper."

Bopa: Local word for 'auntie' – whether a blood relation or a 'Welsh auntie'.

Bosh: The kitchen sink/wash-up; "Have a quick swill in the bosh now before you have your tea".

Botch: Mess, or not very well-completed job; "Don't you get 'im to do it – 'e'll only botch it for you."

Bout of: an attack of, as in, "Every year about this time, somehow or other I do get a nasty bout of 'flue."

Bracchi's: The name often given to the local, Italian-owned café, although the name of the proprietor may well be Rabaiotti or Carpanini.

Brack: Defect, wear and tear; "I've had this frock years and there's still not a brack on it."

Brazen: Impudent in behaviour and impervious to local opinion; "There's a way to carry on – brazen's not the word for it!"

Bread and cheese/Bara caws: The leaves of the hawthorn tree.

Brewer's goitre: A beer-belly.

Brought up under a tub: Raised in a manner leaving much to be desired; "You can't go out in that state – anyone would think you'd been brought up under a tub!"

Butty: (1) A friend or workmate; "We' been big butties/big butts since school."

(2) One of a matching pair; "I can't find the butty to this shoe for the life of me!"

Bwci-bo: Ghost or bogey man.

Bwgi: Head-louse, as in, "When that nurse comes to school she do look for bwgis in ouer 'air."

By: (1) Aside; "You don't have to buy it now, I'll put it by for you."

(2) 'By 'ere' and 'by there' are Wenglish forms of 'here' and 'there'; "Come over by 'ere a minute" and "That's the one youer looking for – over by there".

By you: According to you, as in, "What's the time by you?"

Bucked: Cheered up, encouraged; "… you should have seen him, oh he was bucked when they told him he could start Monday."

C

Came on to me: Accosted; "He came on to me to tell me he found it."

Canting: Gossip, often malicious in nature.

Cack/coggy handed: Left-handed

Calennig: A New Year's gift

Can't abide/Can't stomach/Carn abear: Unable to put up with, as in, "I can't abide/can't stomach/carn abear/it when they show people having operations on the telly."

9

Can't miss him/her: Cannot possibly mistake him/her for someone else; "You can't miss him – he's the one behind the counter – with a little twsh …!"

Calling you: Expected of you "You can have a lie-on in the morning cos there's no calling you is there?"

Cam: Welsh word for a pace or a stride; this word was used in the game of 'catty and doggy' when the striker nominated the number of strides required to pace out the distance back to the 'dab'. Locally, it was always pronounced to sound like 'Calm'.

Cap (keep straight): Keeping someone contented, as in, "We'll afto do as 'e says – better keep 'is cap straight!"

Cap it all: On top of everything; "… and then, to cap it all, after all the fuss we had, the car wouldn't start!"

Carn: Wenglish for can't.

Cart: Carry, as in, "After buying 'eaps of things, we atto cart it all back to the car-Park.".

Case: A comical person; "We do 'ave some fun with all 'is yarns – 'e's a real case, that one!"

Cawl cabbage: A terrible mess, as in, "When them kids 'ad finished playin(g) with theyer toys, it was all cawl cabbage in there!"

Chalk (missed a): Failed to take a chance; "He had every chance to get it, but he missed a chalk there!"

Change (caught on the): A favourite expression of days gone by: "She's just had another baby and she's well in her forties – caught on the change, pooer dab!"

Chesty: Arrogant, boastful; "He's full of himself – a real chesty one!"

Chew bread: To claim close acquaintance (often spuriously or humorously) as in, "… know 'im well, I do! – 'is mother used to chew bread for our ducks!"

Choier: Wenglish for 'choir'.

Choked: So moved as to be unable to speak; "When they gave him his farewell present, he was proper choked"

Choked off: Put in his/her place; "She didn't get anywhere trying to push that rubbish off on me – I soon choked her off!"

Chopping sticks: Cutting firewood

Chopsing/Chopsy: Talking a great deal 'all over the place'. Earning the reputation for being 'a chopsy one'.

Chronic: With no respite from pain; "I was off all night with chronic ear-ache."

Ciff/Cyff: Pronounced 'kiff', (reasonably well), "I thought he was over that bout a sickness, but he don't seem very ciff this morning."

Cilbwt/Crec: Complaint (in medical sense); "He's always got some complaint or other – there's some cilbwt/crec with him all the time!"

Clecs/Carrying clecs: As with the two previous words, from the original Welsh, this time meaning carrying tales about others. A person who made a habit of this was called a 'cleckerbox'.

Clobber: Clothing, belongings, as in, "You are never taking all that clobber – just for the week-end!"

Clodges: Rough pieces of grass with earth attached. Aiming these at others is a fondly-remembered boyhood activity.

remembered boyhood activity.

Clod-hoppers: Heavy, clumsy boots and shoes.

Cocking nose: Behaving disdainfully; " ... putting tidy food for them, and all they do is cock their noses at it – I won't stand for it!"

Cob: (1) To catch the ball in children's games
(2) A 'knot' in one's hair.

Come up a treat: To improve the look of; "This table do come up a treat with a bit of polish."

Come: To get better; "He's been real bard and under the doctor frages, but I think he'll come now."

Coming (no) coming better: To fail to improve in health; "Poor dab, they've tried everything for his complaint, but there's no coming to him."

Compliance (out of): Having lost entitlement; "He've been on the sick so long, he's out of compliance for sick pay now."

Conflab: Wenglish for a lengthy discussion.

Contrary: Awkward, uncooperative; "She's proper contrary, she is – if you only so much as say 'good morning', she'd argue."

Coomb: Wenglish for 'comb'.

Coopy-down: To squat or crouch; see 'twti down' and cwat/quat'.

Cop: (1) Value, as in, "I thought I had a real bargain in this, but there's not much cop to it."
(2) Catch or get, as in, "You'll cop it from your father when he gets home!"

Cop/Cwop: The local Co-operative Society store.

Coppish: Trouser fly; seemingly a derivation of 'cod-piece'.

Cord: Wenglish for 'string'; "Have you got some cord for me to do up this parcel?"

Costa del Hi-ya Butt: A 'tongue-in-cheek' name for Trecco Bay, Porthcawl. It stems from the reputed fact that so many locals used to take holidays there that one was sure to meet many friends and neighbours!

Couple: Rarely meaning 'two' in local usage, more usually a small quantity as in, "Let me have a couple of them apples, please."

Courtin(g) strong: Embarked upon a serious relationship, usually with marriage in mind; "E've 'ad a few girlfriends, but 'im an' that girl 'e's got now are courting strong!"

Crachach: A term to denote the actual, or self-styled gentry.

Craxy: Irritable: "That kid is craxy – he kept us up all night!"

Creatin(g): Going on about, as in, "Last week she was keepin(g) on about 'er shoes – this week, she's creatin(g) about that frock I got 'er"

Credit: Believe, as in, "You wouldn't credit what he called her altogether – gave her the length of his tongue, he did!"

Crib: Wenglish word meaning 'complain'; "He's always cribbing about something or other – there's no pleasing him!"

Crot of a boy: A young lad; from the Welsh 'crotyn', 'crwtyn' or 'crwt' – all words for 'lad'.

Crotchetty: Difficult to live with, pernicketty; "The trouble now is, he's getting old and crotchetty."

Cun: Wenglish for 'can'; "You cun usually find 'im in the club."

11

Cut up: Wenglish for 'upset'. 'distressed'; "Really cut up he was, when he heard about what happened to those kids."

Cute/Cuete: Crafty, cunning; " 'E's cute alright – no flies on 'im!"

Cwat: To hide, conceal.

Cwtch: A much-loved, much used local word having a number of uses:

    (1) The coal cwtch or the cwtch under the stairs/cwtch dan star – a storage place; derived from the Welsh 'cwt'.

    (2) To keep concealed; "Keep that cwtched by there now – don't want nobody to see it"

    (3) Lie down, as in the order to a dog: "Go and (find your) cwtch."

    (4) To be fondled and snuggled in an especially loving way; "Cwtch up to your mam". A child nursed 'Welsh-fashion' is well and truly being 'cwtched'.

    (5) To warn off (now seemingly obsolete in local usage): "Bar cwtch!, bar cwtch!, don't come to my cwtch!" A warning issued by children to others when out blackberry-picking.

Cwtyn y saint: A surviving Welsh expression meaning a dreadfully untidy mess; "Look at the state of this place – its like cwtyn y saint!"

Cythraul/cythral: A devil; another surviving Welsh word.

D

Dai-cap: The flat cap much favoured by colliers in days gone by and still popular locally.

Dab: (1) Creature or thing, as in, "Pooer dab, she do 'ave a lot to put up with with 'im" or "He's won the bingo again, lucky dab!"

    (2) The mark, focal point for the game of 'catty and doggy'.

Dab-hand/dab 'and: Excelling at something; "She's a dab-(h)and with 'er Welshcakes!"

Dad-cu/Tadcu: Usually mutated to 'dacu' with accent on second syllable; the South Wales word for 'grandfather'. North Welsh-people say 'taid'.

Danted/Daunted: At the end of one's tether; "When you think what she gorrw put up with, it's no wonder she do get danted"

Dap it down: To place thoughtlessly; "A course you carn find youer glasses – youer always dappin(g) 'em down without thinkin(g)."

Dap: (1) The same size and shape as; "He's the same dap as his dad exactly."

    (2) An article of footwear for games and P.E.

    (3) Just the right thing; "Just my dap, this is!"

Daro: Probably an euphemism for 'damn'; "Daro, I've just about had all I can take of this"

Deep: Difficult to understand; "The minister's a nice man, but I find his sermons very deep."

Depends (no): Reliability as in, "Goodness knows when he'll turn up – there's no depends on him at all!"

Deuce/Diws/Dukes: An expletive term, a corruption of and euphemism for 'Duw' the Welsh word for 'God'; "O deuce, I've gone and lost it again!"

Didoreth: A Welsh word for which the dictionary offers only the quite inadequate 'feckless' as a meaning. It remains the worst thing that may be said about any local housewife since it means, "There's no shape on 'er round the 'ouse … there's no grain on 'er washing – and 'er 'usband, pooer dab, do afto shift for 'imself!"

Diflas/as diflas as pechod: As miserable as sin; a truly splendid example of mixed translation from Welsh.

Dock: To deduct; "They docked him half a turn for being late."

Dodges: Tricks, ploys, as in, "He's the one to ask about that – he knows all the dodges for sure."

Done in/done up: Tired out; (see 'wanged out')

Done up: (1) Improved, 'tarted up'; "It looks lovely with them now they've had the whole (whool) place done up."

(2) Dressed to kill; "Off she went on 'er date – all done up to the nines"

Don't say stories: Wenglish for 'don't tell lies'

Dose: (1) An attack of an illness, similar to 'bout'; "She've 'ad a nasty dose of 'flue/bronchitis, etc., etc."

(2) To take precautions, as in, "I better dose myself up – I've got a nasty cold coming on, I think."

Dowt: Extinguish a fire/candle, etc. – a good example of an English dialect word found in Wenglish.

Dragged-up: See 'brought up under a tub'

Dravers: Long underwear.

Dribs and drabs: A little at a time, as in, "That's the trouble with them in that shop – only in dribs and drabs they get things in!"

Dust, The: Silicosis, the miners' dreaded disease.

E

Early days yet: Too soon to tell, as in, "It's early days yet to tell – only starting they are, after all …"

Easy: Certainly, without doubt, as in, "I don't know for certain how many were there, but it was easy sixty!"

Echoo (The): An evening paper, widely read in the valleys north of Cardiff.

Eisht/Heisht: Be quiet; a derivation from the Welsh 'Ust!'

'Ell: Not classified under 'H' because, without doubt, 'how the hell' always seems to emerge in local speech as ' 'ow the 'ell', as in, " 'ow the 'ell am I supposed to get down by there?" "It's 'ell of a way off" or "I 'ad 'ell of a job finding them!"

End (no): Abundant, plentiful, as in, "There's no end of bargains to be had in the sales."

Expect: Believe, as in, "They've been there this ages, and it'll be a tidy spell before they get back, I expect."

Eyeful: A small, inadequate amount; "I'm not on a diet now, and you've only given me (an) eyeful of chips!"

F

Fagged out: Tired out, exhausted.

Fair doos: Fair dues, fair play.

Fancy: Think, believe, as in, "I don't know for sure where he's working now, but I fancy he used to work on the line."

Fancying: Wishing, longing for the unattainable; "Only fancying I was! You know I've got strict orders not to eat that!"

Fear (no): In no way! Certainly not! As in, "We told him straight, 'No fear' – not after what happened last time …!"

Feeling: Sympathetic; "You can talk to her; I've always found her very feeling."

Fell it down: Wenglish for 'dropped it'.

Fellum: Wenglish for 'whitlow'. The Welsh word is 'ffelwm'.

Fetching: Attractive, as in, "You're looking very fetching in your new rig-out."

Fidgety: Fussy, pernickety, as in, "My daughter is on to me that I'm too fidgety, but fair play, there's times those kids do get me down."

Fine one: Used in the context of 'People in glass houses shouldn't throw stones'; "You're a fine one to talk, telling him not to do that – you're always doing it yourself!"

First go off: At the very beginning, firstly, as in, "When we got there we went to have a cup of tea, first go off." (See 'last go off/last lap'.)

Fit: Knowing one's way around the system; "She's fit that one – she do get everything that's going!"

Fits, forty: Extreme fright, as in, "When he told me what had happened, I nearly had forty fits!"

Fix, in a: An unenviable state; "I was in a proper fix, I atto get one straight off and none to be had with the shops all shut."

Flag: An unreliable person, as in, "I wouldn't get him to do it – he's a proper flag!" Such a person may be 'a bit of a flag' if deemed to be less than *completely* unreliable

Flighty: A daringly flirtatious woman is always referred to as being 'flighty'.

Fly one: A crafty person; "He's a fly one, making out he didn't know anything about it – and who was the first one there …?"

Forward: Advanced, as in, "Our Sal's little one is really knowing – she's forward for her age."

Frazzle: To the limit, as in, "It was burnt to a frazzle", or, "I'm worn to a frazzle with all I got to do". Another example: "She had worked herself up into a real frazzle."

Fresh: (1) New, extra, as in, "Will you credit it? I've gone and caught a fresh cold on top of the one I had!"

(2) Very cold, as in, "It's fresh this morning, after that frost!"

Frumped: Sulked, as in, "She've been frumpin(g) for a spell now, but leave 'er be – she'll come round, you'll see."

Full fuss: In a state of enthusiasm, as in, "Ages I was, getting them two ready, but now they've gone off, full fuss on their outing!"

Full of it: (1) Exuberant, mischievous, as in, "Look at 'im – like as if 'e was at death's door yesterday – and today, there he is, full of it!"

(2) In the throes of a bad attack of an illness; "I was sure yesterday I was over the worst of this 'flue, but look at me today – full of it again!"

Full pelt: With all speed, as in, "When I told him about it, he was on pins to get there, and then, off he went, full pelt!" (Ianto Full-Pelt is a famous mythical rugby player).

G

Gaffer haulier/Gaffer halier: Usually pronounced to sound like one word, thus 'gafferalier'. It means a boss, someone in charge and is obviously derived from the name given to the man in charge of pit horses.

Gambo: Originally a farm cart, a dray, but used in Wenglish to mean a vehicle which is lacking in refinement and performance; "That car's a bit of a gambo, like!"

Gammy: Lame, as in, "Poor dab, he've still got his gammy leg." Believed by some to be a derivation of the Welsh 'igam-ogam', meaning 'zig-zag'.

Gerraway: A local expression showing disbelief.

Give: (1) Prefer, as in, "Give me shopping there anytime – it's a lot easier."
(6) An unspecified threat; "If you don't behave yourself I'll give you – now, in a minute!"

Giving in: Yielding, as in, "There was one 'ell of a row, but she atto do the giving in, in the end.".

Gip/Gyp: Great pain, as in, "This 'and keeps giving me gyp – it's chronic, honest!"

Glad and sorry: On the 'never never'; glad to have it – sorry to have to pay for it.

Glycereen: The Wenglish pronunciation for 'glycerine'. Another word treated thus is 'paraffin', pronounced 'paraffeen'.

Go by: Rely upon, as in, "You can go by him anytime."

Good: Definite; "There was a good fifty there, I'd say."

Goods: Provisions, as in, "There's not many shops will deliver your goods for you these days!"

Gone: Reached a point; "I'm gone, I don't care any more!" or, "You gorrw admit, she've gone to look proper old lately!"

Gone! Vanished, as in, "When I went to look for it again - there it was – gone!"

Goosegogs: Wenglish for 'gooseberries'.

Gorrw: Wenglish for 'got to'.

Got: Have, as in, "Real nice, it was, when I first had it, but now, I've got no looks on it at all."

Graft: Toil, work, as in, "… bit of hard graft he could do with!"

Grain; A sparkle of cleanliness; "There's a lovely grain on everything with her." From the Welsh 'graen'.

Great: Much used in Wenglish with a long 'a' sound – 'graate', to mean 'splendid'; "We had a graate time – we're really glad we went."

Grizzle: To complain, to moan, as in, "Always grizzlin(g) about something or other, he is – he's a real misery!"

Gummel: To get one's gummel up is to be truly prepared and in the right frame of mind; "Just wait till I get my gummel up – I'll square him!"

15

Gwli: The back of valley houses, providing a possible example of a verbal 'endangered species' since this splendid word does not seem to be heard as much nowadays as once it was. It will surely be a pity if lovely expressions like the following were to disappear: "Those kids of 'ers – comin' in like the road after playing out the back in the gwli!"

H

Half, on: Unfinished, as in, "… they called in while I was busy 'round the house, so I had to leave the work on half."

Half soaked/ 'alf soaked: Slow in movement and/or wit; "He's proper 'alf-soaked – too slow to catch a cold!"

Hammer and tongs: Loudly, passionately; "You could 'ear them 'alf way down the street – quarrelling 'ammer an' tongs, they were!"

Hammering/ 'ammering, a good: A thrashing, as in, "When I get you home, by damn, you're in for a good hammering!"

Had: (1) Tricked; "He thought he had a bargain there, but he was had!"

(2) Available; "I was out of flour to make a bit of cake, and there was none to be had."

Had up: Summoned to appear in court; "He was 'ad up for speeding …"

Hair off/ 'air off: Showing anger; "You dad will 'ave 'is 'air off when 'e sees what you been up to!"

Hand/ 'and, turn 'is: Ability, skill, as in, "Oh, 'e's a tidy feller 'round the 'ouse – turn 'is 'and to anythin(g)"

Hand, in your: (1) A way of having tea; "Will you have a cup of tea in your hand, or will you have it by the table, tidy?"

(2) Readily available; "You can't turn that down – it's money in your hand, really."

Hand's turn/ 'and's turn: Work, as in, " 'E's too tired to gerrout of 'is own way – never does (a) 'and's turn 'round the 'ouse!"

Haze for heat/ 'aze for 'eat: A phrase used by local weather-prophets when assuring you that the early-morning mist will give way to warm sunshine.

Heaps/'eaps: (1) Plenty, a large number; "She put plenty of food for them – there was 'eaps to be 'ad there." Or, "There's 'eaps/loads a people coming to the party."

(2) A good deal, as in, "She've been bard this ages, but she's 'eaps better now."

Heart/ 'eart: Willingness, motivation; "They're so slummocky – I'm gone, I don't 'ave no 'eart to clean the place now."

Heaving/ 'eavin(g): Crowded, as in, "I'm gone. I 'ate all this Christmas shopping – everywhere's 'eavin(g), innit?"

Heavy hand/ 'eavy 'and: Stress and strain, as in, "She've 'ad (a) 'eavy 'and with 'im – nursing 'im all through the winter"

Heavy-handed/ 'eavy 'anded: Liking a lot of, as in, "He's light on milk, but he's heavy-handed on the sugar."

Hec: To hop; this is the Welsh word for this action.

Hewn/ 'ewn: At ease with; another Welsh word.

Highth/ 'ighth: Height; in Wenglish, the word 'height' is treated in the same manner as 'depth'; "That tree you planted is a fair highth/ eyeth now!"

Hikey/ 'ikey: Conceited, stuck up; " 'Ikey bit she is, for sure!"

Hi-ya?/ 'Eye-ya? Seemingly one of the most popular forms of local greeting nowadays, Having supplanted, to a large extent, one-time favourites like, "shw-mae?", " 'owbe?" and "awright?".

Hell: See under " 'ell".

Here's: What awful, as in, "Here's weather – nasty like!!"

Hit him sick/ 'It 'im sick: A dreadful-sounding, often-uttered (but thankfully, rarely-executed) local threat; "There's times I could 'it 'im sick!"

Hobbles: 'Moonlighting', illicit work, as in, " 'E's sposed (supposed) to be on the sick, but 'e's doing a tidy few hobbles."

Hog/ 'og: Extent, as in, "There was no half-measures – we atto go the whole (whool) hog/ 'og."

Holt: Wenglish for 'hold' as in, "He took holt of her coat to stop her from going."

Hop/ 'op, on the: Without preparation, unexpectedly, as in, "Only after breakfast they told us about it – we atto go on the 'op!"

Hopeluss/ 'opeluss: Hopeless

Hopes/ 'opes: Expectations, as in, " 'E's been real bard this ages, but there's 'opes for 'im now…"

Hope in hell/ 'ope in 'ell: No chance at all, as in, "I told 'em to forget it – they 'aven't got (a) 'ope in 'ell!"

How are you fixed?: How are you placed? As in, "They're running a trip to the panto, Tuesday – how are you fixed?"

How (are) you keepin(g): A local enquiry about the state of one's health; "How (are) you keepin(g) these days with all this sicknuss about?"

How are you off for?: How well-provided are you for? Do you need any fresh supplies of?

How do you sell? What price is/are? As in, "How do you sell the apples, eggs, ham, etc., etc."

How's it looking?: What are my prospects? "How's it lookin(g) to borrow a quid?"

Howbe/ 'owbe?: A local greeting.

Hump/ 'ump: Carry; "When you('ve) finished youer shopping, you gorrw 'ump it all back …"

Hunted: Searched, as in, "…I can't think where it can be – I've hunted high and low"

I

I been: Wenglish for 'I have been'; "Porthcawl? – I been there heapsa times/heaps of times" or "I been down the shops, I have."

I could eat him: The ultimate in fondness; "When I see that little dwt sleeping, all cwtched up in bed – Jew, I could eat 'im!"

Ideal/Ideel: Evaporated milk, once very popular for use with 'tin fruete' like 'chunks' (pineapple cubes).

Idle: Out of work, unemployed; *Not* often used locally to mean 'shiftless'.

In a minute: (1) Shortly, presently, as in, "Don't keep on, will you? You shall have it now, in a minute ..."
(2) Willingly; "You should have asked her – she'd have done it for you in a minute!"

Innit? Wenglish for 'isn't it?'

Into everything; Prying into and messing up – cupboards, etc. Much used about young children who have recently learned to walk or crawl; "He's coming on a treat – but he's into everything now!"

It goes through me: It upsets me deeply, as in, "When I see it on the telly, those children – it goes right through me"

'Ighly/highly honoured: Truly privileged, as in, "You can count yourself 'ighly honoured, my lad – she don't let many do that."

Ignorant: Lacking in manners, rather than lacking knowledge.

Is it?: Often used as an interrogative, this is a working translation of the Welsh form; "Going shopping is it?" or, "Having a bit of dinner, is it?"

It's emptying down: "It's raining very heavily" or "It's raining pouring!"

J

Jack: A miner's metal water jug.

Jack it in: To give up a pursuit or hobby, as in, "I've just (almost) had a bellyful of that – I'll have to jack it in!"

Jant: Wenglish for a jaunt, an outing.

Jawch/Jawl: A Wenglish expletive; "Jawl/jawch, mun, there's no need for language like that!" These words are mutations of the Welsh word for 'devil' – 'diafol'.

Jest/Just; Nearly, as in, "I can tell you, I'm jest going mad with this toothache!"

Jew!: A euphemism of the Welsh 'Duw' (God); "Jew, there's bard he's looking!" or "Jew, there's old she've gone to look lately!"

Jib: Looks, facial features, as in, " 'E's the same jib as 'is dad, exactly."

Jibs: Pulling faces, as in, "If you don't stop making them jibs, people will think you're not all there!"

Jibbed: Failed to keep a promise; "He promised faithful he'd do it, but at the last minute, he jibbed. Let me down rotten, he did!"

Jinny: A home-based, punishment cane – happily a word from the past.

Job: Bother, trouble "There's a job we had finding shoes to fit him" or "You'll have a job on with that!"

Job, bad: A lost cause; "I've tried my level best with it, but in the end, I atto give it up as a bad job"

Jocose: Comfortable, at ease, as in, "You're looking real jocose, lying down by there!"

Joking: Artificial, as in, "They didn't have real flowers – only jokin(g) ones ..."

Just!: Really! As used to show complete agreement with something said about someone else – " 'Aven't she just!"

Jubes: Wenglish for 'fruit pastilles'.

K

Keepin(g) on: Making constant reference to; "I thought he was happy about it, but now, he's keepin(g) on all the time."

Keep short: Deprive, as in, "She don't have a great deal of money to play with when she've paid her way – they say he keeps her pretty short!"

Ketch: Catch, usually used with 'holt'; "You gorrw ketch holt of it tight …"

Kidney beans: Runner beans.

Knock about with: Keep company with; " 'E' do knock about with a funny lot, I cun tell you!"

Kokum: Crafty, cunning, as in, " 'E's kokum that one – 'e do get away with murder 'alf the time!"

Know for: Know the whereabouts of, as in, "I know for your shoes – they are upstairs."

L

Lambasting/Lamping: A good hiding: "You're asking for a good lambasting/lamping if you don't watch it!"

Landed: In one's element; "Give 'im something to potch with, and 'e's landed …"

Last go off/Last lap: At the very end, as in, "I reminded him to put the cat out, last go off/last lap."

Learn: Wenglish for 'teach'; the Welsh word 'dysgu' is used to mean both 'learn' and 'teach'.

Let himself/herself go: Not keeping up appearances; " 'E've let 'imself go since 'is wife died, you can tell"

Let loose; Acting in a wild manner; "Behave yourself, will you? – you're acting like as if you're let loose."

Lick, a tidy: At a good pace; "They've nabbed him again for speeding – he must have been going a tidy lick!"

Lie on: Stay in bed later than usual; "I can have a lie on in the morning because it's Saturday."

Life, got to be for my: Having to be alert; "There's no knowing what he'll be up to next – I gorrw be for my life with him!"

Like a good 'un: As well as ever, as in, "Lately 'e've been off 'is food, but 'e's eating like a good 'un again."

Like a lath: Very thin; "She's been on that diet this ages and lately, she've gone like a lath/as thin as a lath."

Like a shot: Without delay, as in, "I only had to ask him the once – he did it like a shot, fair play!"

Line, on the: On the railway, as in, "He used to work on the line, for sure."

19

Livin(g) tally: Co-habiting without benefit of clergy; "They've been livin(g) tally ever since 'er 'usband cleared off."

Look-in: The faintest, outside chance, as in, "He thought he was a cert for that job, but when it came to, he didn't even have a look-in."

Looking: Giving an appearance of, as in, "It's looking nice with you, now you've had the place done up!"

Looking daggers; Giving disapproving looks.

Look-out: Prospect: "It's a poor look-out for them now, since he's been made redundant."

Looks: Right feelings for, as in, "It's no good, since I've had it cleaned, I've got no looks on it now."

Loose go!: Wenglish for 'Let go!' 'Release it!' This command may also be, 'Leave go!', 'Leave it go!' or, 'Let go of it!'

Losing on oneself: Becoming almost permanently moithered, confused; "She's gone, she can't remember a thing – I think the poor dab is losing on herself – must be her age!"

Losins/Loshins: Sweets, from the Welsh.

Lost the bus: Missed the bus – a translation of the Welsh expression.

Lot: A good deal, often as in, "I like this new coat – I wear a lot of it!"

Lump: Big, as in, "He's a real lump of a boy – got to have his school clothes made special for him."

M

Maldod/Muldod: Indulgence, spoiling, as in, "He's gone to live away now, but he's home often for a bit of muldod." 'Maldod' is a Welsh word.

Mamgu/Myngu: Usually pronounced 'mungee' – grandmother. 'Mamgu is the South Wales word for grandmother. 'Nain' is preferred in North Wales.

Mandrel: The local word for a pick.

Mark, left its: Effect, as in, " 'E've been real bard and it 'ave left its mark on 'im now"

Mary Jane: Effeminate; "He's a nice enough feller but he's a bit of a Mary Jane, of course."

Match, like a: Very quick tempered; "Watch how you talk to him – like a match, he is!"

Mind out: Take care, beware; "Mind out – you nearly hit that over!" or "Mind that by there – move it, can't you?" or "Mind that out of the way!"

Mingy: Mean, stingy, as in, "They're proper mingy in that shop – only give you (a) eyeful a sweets for ten pence."

Minute, in a: Later on, not as immediate as it sounds; "You'll have to wait – I'll let you have them in a minute.!"

Mitching: Wenglish for playing truant.

Mob: Hide and seek.

Moch/Mockers/Molochi: Ruining, spoiling as in, "You've put the moch/mockers/molochi on that fire proper with all that small coal …"

Moithered: Confused, uncertain, as in, "I can't take a crowd of them coming now, I do get moithered, like ..."

Morv: Wenglish for 'mauve'.

Most probably/most probly: Almost certainly; "He's most probably/probly with his brother up the club."

Mouthful: A good deal of cheek; "They won't take a blind bit of notice of what I do say – when I do tell 'em off, all I do get is a mouthful!"

Muffler: A scarf, not of the flimsy type.

Murder, half: A local threat, "I'll 'alf murder you if I get my hands on you!"

N

Nasty: Severely, as in, "Take your umbrella with you because it might come on to rain nasty."

Neely: Wenglish for 'nearly'

Never: (1) An expression showing complete disbelief; "Is that what he told you? *Never!*"

(2) A firm denial; "Did I take them? – no, I never!"

Never right: Having something seriously wrong, as in, "I've told him and told him, till I'm blue in the face, but he's still at it – he's never right, for sure!"

Niblo: A word used locally for a young, male member of the family; "Keep youer eye on Niblo and see what he's up to."

Nines, up to: To the limit, as in, "She fancies her chances, she do – always done up to the nines, even when she's not going anywhere."

Noise, a big: Someone of importance, as in, "He's a big noise with the Legion/Buffs/ Masons."

Nothing for: Not very partial to, as in, "I got a real soft spot for pikelets, but I'm nothing for rice pudding."

Not much to play with: Not a great deal of surplus cash; "By the time I've paid my way, there's not much to play with, I can tell you."

Now jest: Later on, as in, "I won't take them now, I'll have them now jest." See 'again/agen'. Sometimes used to mean 'a short while ago'; "... now, what was I saying now jest ...?"

Now: Rarely used to mean 'immediately'; "I'll be going up to Murrayfield for the match now, next month," or "I'll see to it now, when I get home."

***Now* I'm coming:** It's only now that I've arrived; "*Now* I'm coming down here! – it's shameful them buses!!"

O

Odd: Plus, as in, "I've only got a pound odd on me."

Of going: Since I was already going; " ... so, of going to Ponty, I thought I'd get a few things from the market."

Off: (1) Going to, as in, "Where (are) you off this morning?" or "I'm off home now." Or "Where (are) you off to?"

(2) Angry, upset; "He'll be off when he hears about that."

(3) On the go; "That baby is proper craxy again – had us off all night with him, he did."

Off sick: Away from work due to ill-health.

Off (h)is 'ead: Behaving strangely, showing signs of mild derangement.

Off with: Having a disturbed time; "He had a nasty smack at work, and last night he was off with his shoulder all night ..."

Oil cloth: A fondly remembered word from childhood, meaning 'linoleum'.

Oils, in his: In his element; "Give 'im a book to bury 'is 'ead in an' 'e's in 'is oils ..."

Old: Strange; "Funny old day, innit?" or "Funny old stick he is."

On: (1) Belonging to; "There's some paws on that dog!"

(2) About, as in, "Don't call names on people!"

Both these examples show the influence of the original Welsh way of saying these things

On a course of tablets/tabluts: Many Wenglish speakers like to give their ailments a certain significance so that, instead of saying merely that they have been prescribed pills or drugs, they prefer, "I was under the doctor and he put me on a course of tabluts."

On me: In my possession, as in, "I'll have to pay you again – I don't have enough on me now."

On (h)is own: A humorous, comical character; " 'E's a real scream – 'e's on 'is own"

On pins: Agitated; "Nothing's too 'ot or too 'eavy for 'im – I'm on pins with 'im 'alf the time."

On the go: In course of preparation; "When they asked me to come over for a bit of dinner I told them it was too late, my dinner was already on the go"

On the road: Outside; "Your father will be here soon, he's just talking to someone on the road" or "The only time I ever see her is when I meet her on the road."

On the sick; Receiving sick benefit money.

On the trot: Consecutively; "It's funny how the same thing's happened to me three days on the trot."

'Ope in 'ell: The remotest chance; " 'E thinks 'e's OK for the driving test, but in my opinion 'e 'aven't got (a) 'ope in 'ell."

Open tap: The commencement of licensing hours; "Jew, when's open tap 'round 'ere? I got a thirst I wouldn't sell for a quid!"

Opening medicine: Local expression meaning 'laxative'.

Or no: Or not; "I don't know for certain if 'e'll be going or no."

Ouer/Ouers: Wenglish for 'our' and 'ours', also 'hour'.

Out of: Without, as in, "Sorry, we're out of them, but we'll be having some in now, in an hour or so."

Outings: Problems, as in, " 'E's a real 'andful – we do 'ave some outings with 'im, I cun tell you."

22

Overcoat colder: Considerably colder; "Damn aye, it's (an) overcoat colder in Merthyr than down Cardiff – and (an) overcoat and muffler colder in Brynmawr!"

P

Packman: An itinerant salesman.

Packman's puzzle: A street or housing estate where the house-numbers, allocated in a complicated fashion, cause problems to visitors, tradesmen, etc.

Paish: Literally, from the Welsh word for 'petticoat', but used to suggest effeminacy; "he's a nice chap, but a bit of a paish"

Pass the time of day: To exchange pleasantries when meeting friends and acquaintances; "He was in a hurry but he managed to pass the time of day with me."

Pishti/pishty: Possibly a derivation of 'paish.'

Palaver: Fuss and bother, as in, "He's done it this time, for sure – there'll be lot of palaver about it."

Parading: Back and forth; "He was in and out of bed all night parading to the toilet."

Passed very high: Possessing good academic qualifications; "Their youngest got a good head on 'im – passed very high, you know!"

Pat, black: Wenglish for 'cockroach'.

Patch, not a: Not to be compared with, as in, "These cakes are not a patch on the ones last week.."

Pay your way: To meet one's commitments; "By the time I've paid my way, there's nothing left"

Pelting: (1) Raining heavily.
　　　　　(2) Throwing stones, etc.

Pewer: Wenglish for 'pure'.

Picking rain: Beginning to rain; "It's picking rain again," or "It's picking to rain". This word from 'pigan', the Welsh word meaning 'starting to rain'.

Picking up with: Getting into company with; "They picked up with some nice people on holiday."

Picking up on: Criticising; "She's always pickin(g) me up on the way I do talk."

Pickings: Selection, choice, as in, "By the time I got to the jumble sale, all the best pickin(g)s were gone."

Pics: Welsh-cakes; from the Welsh, 'Picau ar y maen' (on the stone).

Piece: (1) A young woman; "Have you met his new girl-friend? – tidy piece she is!"
　　　　(2) A round of bread and butter.

Pikelet: A much-enjoyed South Wales tea-time treat which might be described as a 'drop scone'. The word is a derivation of 'bara-pysglyd' (pitchy bread).

Pinking up: To make oneself ready, to titivate; (from the Welsh).

Pisio cath/pisio crics: Very weak tea.

Pitch in: (1) To set to with a will; "I atto leave myself plenty of time to catch the bus, so I was up early and pitched in with my work first go off."
　　　　　(2) Get on with eating; "You must be starving – pitch in, there's heaps for

everybody!"

Pitched a tale: Told an improbable story; "More fool 'er! 'E pitched 'er a tale about why 'e was late – and she swallowed it!"

Playing the bear with: Causing a good deal of pain/suffering/bother; "This weather do play the bear with me …"

Plod: Wenglish pronunciation of 'plaid', as in, "She looks very smart in her Scotch plod rig out."

Potch: (1)   A mixture of potato and swede. The Welsh word is 'ponsh maib'.

(2)   To mess about with, as in, "He's always potchin(g) with something or other in that shed of his out the back."

(3)   Trouble, as in, "She's forever in some potch or other about something."

Pouring, raining: Rather than say, "It's pouring with rain", many Wenglish speakers prefer, "It's raining pouring!" or "It's pouring down."

Proper: Interchangeable with 'real', meaning 'definite', as in "Don't give it to him to do – he's a proper flag!"

Puff, out of: Out of breath; "She was out a puff when she got there because she'd been rushing up the trip."

Pug: Looking less than clean, in need of a wash; "There's pug you're looking – have you had a tidy wash?" From the Welsh 'pyglyd' meaning 'like pitch'.

Pull: (1)   A bout of, as in, "This morning again, he had another nasty pull of coughing."

(2)   To climb, as in, "They live right on top – it's one hell of a pull to get there!"

Pulled about: Messed up, disarranged; "I hate the place all pulled about when you are having the (chimney) sweep."

Pulled to pieces: Very severely criticised; "The teacher pulled her to pieces about the way she was carrying on."

Put: (1)   Place, as in, "When she told me that, it shook me rigid – I didn't know where to put myself for a minute."

(2)   Provide, as in, " … and of course, I put tea for all of them"

(3)   Serve with; "Put me a couple of them pears, please."

Putickler/particular: (1)   Fussy, as in, "Very putickler about his food he is"

(2) In question, as in, "Well, as I was saying, this particular man was looking for his butty ."

Put oneself straight: Smarten oneself up; "Tell her I'll be up now in a minute – as soon as I've put myself straight, like."

Q

Quat: To squat, or crouch. The Welsh word is 'cwat'. (See 'twti-down' and 'coopy-down'.)

Quavers: Pronounced 'quarvers' to mean a trembling in the voice, as in, "She've got a nice enough little voice, but there's all of them quarvers in it!" Also used for affectations in the voice.

Queenie/Queenie ball: A children's ball game

Quid: Originally a guinea, then a pound.

Quids in: Well off, as in, "Since he got a job there, he's quids in."

Quite, not: Not really, as in, " 'E 'aven't quite got the 'ang of it yet!"

R
Rainin(g) nasty: Raining very heavily.

Rampin(g): Very painful, as in, "She've been up all night with toothache, rampin(g)!"

Rared: Wenglish pronunciation of 'reared'; "She wasn't brought up 'round 'ere – rared by 'er auntie she was!"

Radically wrong: Very wrong: "There's something radically wrong with this – I can't make it go for love or money."

Raise: To take up; "Before I could make a start on the work I atto raise the ashes." A translation of the Welsh.

Rather: Prefer, as in, the oft-repeated, "Pink I do like, but blue I do rather." Also, "I'd much rather …"

Really/Reelly speaking: In actual fact; "It looks like a Corgi but really speakin(g) it's a mongrel"

Read: Examined, as in, "You're daft, you are – you want your head read!"

Regular/Reg'ler: Regularly, as in, " 'E's one of the lucky ones, I reckon – 'e's days reg'ler, top pit."

Ribblin(g)s: Cinders, the end-product of using a 'ribber'/sieve on the remains of a spent fire. The ribbings, often mixed with small coal, provide 'banking' for many a fire.

Right enough: Definitely right.

Right as rain: Fit, as in, "She had a nasty cough last week, but she's right as rain now again."

Right-o: Used to express agrement, to show willingness; "Right-o then, tell her I'll be up now" The alternative to this, is 'Right you are, then'.

Right off: (1) Straightaway, as in, "I won't hang about with this – I'll do it right off for you."

(2) Completely, as in, "I've had a sickener of beans – I'm gone right off them now."

Rig-out: Outfit; "I like youer new rig-out … very nice indeed – that style's all the rage now …"

Rise: (1) Purchase; "I just had time to rise my ticket before the train came in."

(2) Commence; "The funeral will rise from the house at two o'clock". Both these examples show the Welsh expression has been translated literally.

Road, any: In any case, as in, "… any road, I wouldn't go now – even if they asked me."

Road, like the: Very dirty; "…coming in here like the road after potching out the back – *ach-y-fi!*"

Rodney: A disreputable person. The last train up the valleys from places like Cardiff and Newport was once called "The Rodney's".

Rolling in it: Having it in abundance; " 'E don't give much money when they come 'round collecting – an 'e's rolling in it!"

Ronk: Dyed in the wool, arrogant; "It's no good arguing with him – he's a ronk Communist!" The Welsh word for this is 'rhonc'.

Rose up his/her sleeve: Encouraged, urged on; "For shame on you – he's in real

25

trouble now – and you rose up his sleeve all through!"

Ructions: A good deal of 'palaver' and bother, usually noisy, as in, "You've been told 'eaps of times about that – an' you've done it again – there'll be ructions when youer father gets in!"

Rotten: Badly, as in, "He promised faithful – and here it is again – he've let me down rotten!"

Rough: Not really well, as in, "Damn, aye mun, I feel rough this mornin(g)."

Rue-bob: Wenglish for 'rhubarb'.

Ruined: Badly-spoiled; "Ruined, 'e is, right enough – she spoils 'im rotten!!"

Rush you: Charge, as in, "I like youer 'at – 'ow much did they rush you for that?"

S

Salty: Expensive: "I was after one o those videos but it was too salty for me, so I had to leave it where it was."

Samwidge: Wenglish for 'sandwich'.

Scent: The local word for 'perfume'.

Scholarship, The: The name by which the 11-plus was once known.

See is she in: See if she is in; "Knock the door and see is she in."

Send on: See off; "I couldn't send her on the bus, but I sent her a bit of the way."

Scrammed: Wenglish for 'scratched'

Screch: Screech; another surviving Welsh word. It is also used to denote a disagreeable person; "Proper old screch she is!"

Screw: (1) Wages, salary. It used to be said that someone was getting 'a good screw' for his work. For obvious reasons it cannot be used today without being quite misunderstood!

(2) Pronounced in the Welsh manner with an open sound to the 'e' as in 'egg'. It means a sharp-tongued woman, a shrew; "Real old screw, she is – nothing good to say about anyone."

Serchus: Not used to mean 'pleasant' or agreeable as this Welsh word really suggests, but in a sarcastic manner to denote a miserable person; "Look out, here comes old serchus!"

Shame, for: As in standard English, but always accompanied by 'for'; "For shame on you, carrying on like that!"

Shandivang/Shandibang: In a dreadful mess; "When he had finished wilmuntin in my chest of drawers, it was all shandivang!"

Shape: (1) System, or fashion; "There's no shape on 'er 'round the 'ouse!" Or "It was hard work, but I managed it some shape." Or "I tried my best but the same shape it was when I finished."

(2) Stir, bestir; "Shape yourself, will you! – we're off now in a minute!"

Sharp: (1) Sternly, as in, "If 'e don't take no notice, I'll afto speak sharp to 'im."

(2) Cold, as in, "It's a sharp one this morning!"

(3) 'On the ball', clever; "You carn fool 'im – 'e's a sharp one!"

(4) Cheat; one who cheats at cards is a 'card-sharp.'

Shook rigid: Greatly surprised, shocked; "It shook him rigid when they gave him his cards for being late again."

Siop/Shop popeth: A Welsh expression for a general store, a shop that sells 'everything'.

Sinking: Longing for: "When we got back after taking the dog out, I was sinking for a cup of tea."

Sinking fast: Spoken in hushed tones when I was young, it showed the final abandonement of hope in a serious illness; "Poor dab, there's no hopes for him – he's sinking fast "

Sharpish: Quickly, as in, "They'll be here before long now, I better make some cake sharpish."

Sioni/Shwni Dai: One whose dress leaves much to be desired, as in, "Haven't you got something tidy to wear? – you look a proper Sioni Dai in them old things."

Sioni/shwni bob ochr: A surviving Welsh expression meaning someone who 'runs with the hare and hunts with the hounds'. Literally , 'Johnny all sides'.

Shift: Manage, as in, "She's 'opeluss 'round the 'ouse and 'er kids afto shift for themselves."

Skew-whiff/wiff: Awry, askew, as in, "You haven't hung that picture straight – it's all skew-wiff with you"

Skulkin(g): Surreptitious and illicit visits to the pantry.

Slap it off: Wear too often, as in, "Take youer new coat off – musn't slap it off, you need something for best!"

Sledge; (1) A measurement of daftness, as in, "I don't know what to make of him – he's as twp as a sledge these days!"

(2) Stupidly; "I don't know what comes over her sometimes – there's times she do talk like a sledge!"

Sleish/Sly-sh: A small shovel; used for coal, cinders etc.

Slouch hat: Wenglish for 'trilby hat'.

Slummocky: Not as bad as 'didoreth' – but almost! "She've always been slummocky – there's not much shape on her!"

Smack: An accident, particularly in the pit.

Smack in front: Directly, as in, "When you get there, you'll see the shop you're after – smack in front of you."

Smack in the chops: A disappointment, as in, " … she didn't get it after all – real smack in the chops, that was!"

Small, small: The Welsh habit of using a double adjective is echoed in Wenglish, so that one hears, "Oh it was small, small – you could hardly see it." One also hears about 'a small, little man' or 'a big 'uge factory'.

Small beer: A herbal drink remembered with great affection from childhood – does anyone make this 'nectar' nowadays?

Soc, in a: Unconscious, as in, "She's not taking any notice, that girl behind the counter – must be in a soc, or something!"

Sorry (in) his/her heart: Extremely sorry for, as in, "When 'e told 'er about all the bother 'e'd been in, she was sorry (in) 'er 'eart for 'im."

So there for you!: That's it!; "That's all you're getting, so there for you!"

Sparkin(g): Local word for courting

Spec, on: In hopeful anticipation, as in " ... only went there on spec, we did!"

Spell: A period of time, as in, " ... and after being on the line, I had a spell down the pit."

Spiteful: Unwilling, as in, "Sorry the fire's slow coming – being spiteful it is!"

Spouting: Talking; "Where's he off spouting tonight, then?"

Spragged: Tripped; " 'E spragged 'imself when 'e trood (trod) on 'is own coat, bending down" A sprag was used in the colliery; it was a bar (cog-stick) inserted in dram (tram) wheels to stop them running backwards. This led to another local expression, "I soon put a sprag in that!" ('I soon put a stop to that!')

Sprateus: Another word for a sharp-tongued person.

Sprottin(g)/Sprwtin: Prying and interfering; of Welsh origin?

Spreathed: Chapped by cold weather.

Spuds: Holes in stockings.

Square: Deal with "any more of 'is nonsense and I'll square 'im I will!"

Star turn: A comical or whimsical person; " ... the things he comes out with – he's a star turn!"

Stick: Person; "You never know where you are with him – funny old stick, he is."

Stitch, every whip: With monotonous regularity; "I don't like to pass remarks but there's no peace to be had – he's rouind here every whip-stitch!!"

Stoptap: When the pubs and clubs close.

Straight: In a direct manner "I've had just about as much as I can take, and I told her straight!"

Stroke: Anything at all; " ... 'elp 'er? – 'e don't do a stroke, if 'e can 'elp it!"

Stroke, alter: Improve; "You'll afto alter youer stroke, my lady, when you start that new job ..."

Struck: Impressed, as in, "I went to the sales as usual, but I wasn't struck with anything there!"

Stump: The core of an apple; "Mingy, he is – didn't even leave me the stump!"!

Suck-in; Disappointment: "He had a real suck-in with that – he thought he was going to walk it!"

Swanky: An example of a word which is now 'an endangered species'. Thirty years ago, a local person, impressed by something said, would almost certainly have said, "Oh, there's swanky!" Nowadays, the response will surely be, "Oh, there's posh!" The word 'swank' is still to be heard, however.

Swansea: A much-enjoyed local loaf of bread.

Swill: (1) Empty and rinse the teapot.

(2) Have a quick wash, as in, "You better swill youer hands in the bosh before youer dinner."

There is a gradation of various 'swills' which one may have in the bosh: you can:

(a) swill your hands

(b) have a quick swill ('a cat's lick and a promise)

(c) have a tidy swill (a good wash)

Tack: Produce; used in a derisory sense to mean 'inferior; "Fancy buying that cheap tack" or "I won't have any of that old foreign tack in this house."

Taffy: The old Wenglish word for 'toffee'.

Tampin(g) mad: Very angry; "Tampin(g) mad, he was, after seeing how they were carrying on – and usually, he won't say boo nor ba(h) to anyone about anything!!"

Tamping (ball): Bouncing.

Tapped: (1) Repaired, as in, "You(d) better have your shoes tapped before you go back to school."

(2) 'Not all there'; " 'E do say some peculiar things – there's sometimes I think 'e's a bit tapped. "

Taw: A child's best marble; the one with which you aim at other marbles.

Tawch: An unpleasant taste, tainted; "Mam, there's a funny tawch on this butter". The Welsh word 'tawch' literally means a haze or fog.

Tea-fight/bun fight: An old expression for a free meal – usually at chapel.

Teisen/teeshen lap: A simple, easily-prepared fruit cake.

Thank you (I wouldn't give): Not liking, as in, "I wouldn't give thank you for rice-pudding now – I've gone right off it!"

Thar wun: Wenglish for 'that one'.

There's a price on: How awful! "There's a price on everything these days!"

There's nice/lovely/posh, etc.: How nice/lovely/posh; "There's nice you've got it now, after doing the whool (whole) place up!" Another variation is "There's posh for you!" Such expressions are a direct translation from the Welsh form.

There's times: There are occasions, as in, "There's times I could cry when I stop to think about it all."

There you are then: That's it; "Well, there you are then – it's finished at last!" This, too, is a direct translation from Welsh.

There's some weather we're having: 'Some' in this instance may be used to mean 'awful'/'unusual'/'wet'/'stormy', etc.

These days: Nowadays, currently, as in, "Say what you like, you don't seem to get nice jaffas these days."

Thick, a bit: A bit much, as in, "It's a bit thick, innit, expecting me to turn round and put tea for all of them!"

Threw it up: Reminded in an unpleasant way; "She won't let go of it – last week again, she threw it up to me again."

Through and through: (1) Sharing someone's house without having specific separate rooms (see 'apartments'). "It's awkward asking anyone to come, see – we're living through and through."

(2) Lumps and small coal mixed together, unsieved.

Tidy: One of the most over-worked Wenglish words, as the following examples show:
Tidy! – fine, splendid;
A tidy spell – quite a long time;
A tidy few – quite a number;
A tidy feller – a decent chap, probably 'good with his hands'.
A tidy step, back and fore – quite a long way.
"Talk tidy!" – "Speak properly!"
A tidy swill – a wash, involving at least face *and* hands.
A tidy bit in the bank – plenty of money; 'filthy-wealthy'.

Tight: In short supply, especially money.

Tight-fisted: Mean

Time, in no: Swiftly; "I bought three in the sales, in no time!"

Tin-tacks: Small nails, sometimes drawing pins.

To, where's it: Where is it?

To be: In my possession, in being; "I've found five of them, but I'm sure there's another one to be, somewhere."

Tommy-box: The collier's food container.

Tossel: Often, the preferred Wenglish pronunciation of 'tassel'.

Toy: A 'character' as in, " 'E's a real toy – always some old nonsense or other with him!"

Trailer: Wenglish for 'caravan'; "They've got a *bewtiful* trailer down Trecco!"

Trewth: Truth.

Tricks, how's: A local greeting; "Hi-ya kid/'I-ya kid – (h)ow's tricks?"

Trimmings: Christmas decorations; locally, we 'trim-up' for Christmas.

Trip: (1) An outing.
(2) A hill, or a rise, as in, "You'll soon get out a puff if you go up that trip."

Troughing: Roof-guttering.

Tump: A small hill.

Turn: (1) Proceed, as in, "I'm gone, I don't know which way to turn."
(2) Time, as in, "This will do another turn or so. "Possibly, this is an adaptation of the Welsh idiom "Fe wnaiff y tro hwn eto"."
(3) A shift at work; "Steady feller, he is – he hasn't lost a turn this ages."

Turn (h)is (h)and: Manage to do well; "Tidy feller, 'e is! – turn 'is 'and to anythin(g)!"

Turn round: Follow up with; "On top of everything, I had to turn round and put supper for six of them!"

Turned it over: Changed TV channels; "I wasn't struck with anything on BBC so I turned it over to the other side."

Twang: An affected accent, as in, "She've got a twang you could cut with a knife!!"

Twelvemonth/Twelmunth: One year; "It's hard to credit it, but I been drawing my pension for neely a twelmunth – it'll be a whool twelmunth now, in April."

Two, make two of: Much larger than; " 'E's only a little dwt – an' she's a real boilin(g) piece – make two of 'im, she would!"

Twp/twpsyn: A little slow on the uptake, not really *very* dull; "She's a bit twp this morning after being up all night, but usually she's as bright as a button." A person who is habitually slow may well be called 'a bit of a twpsyn'. The ultimate is, "twp as a sledge" because you "talk like a sledge".

Twt/dwt: Small in stature, a young child; "What can you expect – only a little dwt she is, after all!" Another Welsh expression.

Twti-down: To crouch, to squat. (See 'coopy down' and 'cwat'.) 'Twti' is a Welsh term.

Twll of a place: A very poor place; "I wouldn't give thank you to live in a twll of a place like that!" 'Twll' is the Welsh word for 'hole'.

Twsh: A small moustache.

Ty-bach; The lavatory.

U

Under my feet: In the way; "Since he's been retired, I can't seem to get on with my work like I used to – under my feet all day, he is!"

Under the doctor: A delightful local expression meaning under the doctor's care; " 'E've been bard alright – 'e've been under the doctor this ages, but I think he's coming now."

Under the weather: Not feeling too well.

Up all night: Having had a disturbed night; "Up all night, I was – with fidgety pains in my legs"

Up together: Well-organised, as in, " … you wouldn't take them for two sisters – one's a bit wit-wat and the other one's always up together."

Up to the mark: (1) When you don't feel 'up to the mark' you are not as well as you might be, although the actual cause is probably not clear.

(2) Up to the expected standard, as in, "These pillow slips are not up to the usual mark, but they know how to charge for them!"

W

Wanged/Wanged out: Exhausted, tired out; "I don't seem to have much go in me these days, I'm as weak as a robin and I'm wanged out by tea-time."

'Ware-teg: Fairplay, an adaptation of the Welsh 'chwarae-teg', which shows the South Walian (monoglot and Welsh-speaking) reluctance to use the 'ch' sound.

Washes like a rag: 'Comes up a treat' after every washing, to the evident delight of local housewives.

Wass/wuss; Lad, not manservant, as suggested by the Welsh word from which it is derived, 'gwas'.

Watch points: Study the situation before taking action, as in, "Watch points by 'ere now, then you'll get the 'ang of it!"

Weddol/Gweddol: A possible reply to, "How are you feeling today?" The Welsh word 'gweddol' means 'fair'.

Went in for: Decided to proceed with, as in, "They waited a couple of years before they went in for a family/house/car", etc.

Wfft!: Originally used, as the original Welsh intends, to mean "Shame on them!" but is also used – more rudely – to mean something like "Sucks to them!"

Whiff/Wiff: A short rest; "I was out of puff from hurrying so I had a bit of a whiff on the seat."

Whimberries/Wimberries: The local word for the succulent fruit picked by dedicated enthusiasts in late summer.

Wimuntin/Wilmentan/Chwilmantan: Versions of the Welsh word meaning 'to pry'. In local usage, it means not only to pry but also to proceed to rummage about. "When that kid of 'ers 'ad finished wimuntin in my cupboards, it was all shandivang!"

Winky, in a/like a: Very quickly; " 'E gave me a real mouthful an' was out of the 'ouse like a winky before I could cop 'old of 'im."

'Witched: Bewitched: "There's weather we're having – must be 'witched, I think!"

Wit-wat: Unable to be depended upon, inconsistent, as in, "Oh, she's wit-wat, gul, she do say one thing an' then do something different altogether ..." The Welsh 'chwit-chwat' means 'fickle'.

With your finger in your mouth: Without the required means, as in, "You'll have to find some money for the outing – you can't go there with your finger in your mouth!"

Wonky: Defective; "That new car of his is wonky, for sure – he's back and fore to the garage with it every whip-stitch."

Wossname: Wenglish form of 'whatsisname'.

Wise, awake before: Rising early, as in, "He's up early every morning, reg'lar – an if you ask me, he's awake before he's wise, most mornings ..."

Wrap up warm!: An injunction to put on warm clothing before braving cold weather.

Wyer: Wenglish for 'wire', similarly, 'fyer', 'lyer', etc.

Wy-luss: Wireless, radio; "I could kick myself – coming out without my mac – it said on the wyluss to expect rain today – makes you feel such a fool getting caught like this."

Y

Yarn: A good joke, as in, "Anybody know any good yarns? We could do with a laugh."

Yearins: Wenglish for 'earrings'.

Years: Wenglish for 'ears'

Years, this: For many a long day; "It's not a new outfit – I've had it this years!"

Yelling blue murder: Crying and 'carrying on' to maximum effect; "Upset's not the word for it – yelling blue murder, she was!!"

Yorks; The practice of tying colliers' and other workmen's trousers above the ankles to prevent dirt and dust reaching the upper parts of the body.

Youer: Wenglish for both 'your' and 'you're'.

Items of the *'News in Wenglish'* series broadcast on Radio Wales.

These items are given, first in Standard English, then in their Wenglish 'translations'.

A snatch of conversation between two ladies meeting in Cardiff:

"Hullo, Glad, how nice to see you."
"Hullo, Val, how are you – I'm surprised to see you down here!"
"I came down for the sales with Trisha; we decided to come at the last minute."
"How did it go?"
"There were plenty of bargains; but what I was really looking for was a handbag to match my new suit, but I couldn't find anything suitable anywhere."
"Did you get your dress in Howells' sale?"
"No, I've this dress for some years – a real bargain – it washes so well – and still looks as good as new."
"I bought a lovely one last year, but I had to have it cleaned – and this was not a success – I hardly wear it now ..."

Wenglish:

"Hi-ya, Glad, there's nice to see you."
" 'Ullo there, Val., 'ow's tricks gul – fancy seein' you down by 'ere!"
"Came down for the sales with ouer 'Trish – came on the 'op, we did!"
" 'Ow did you get on?"
"Found a tidy few bargains – I came down special for a new 'ambarg to go with my new rig-out – but there was nothing to suit in the whool place."
"Did you get youer frock in Howellses sale?"
"No, gul, I've 'ad this one this years – a real cop it was – it do wash like a rag – and there's still not a brack in it!"
"I bought a *bewty* last year, but I atto 'ave it cleaned – and they made a real mess of it for me. I've got no looks on it now!"

Although Mary said she had nothing suitable to wear, she agreed to go on an excursion with her Aunt Annie. It was hastily arranged and they bought their tickets at short notice. When they arrived, they decided to look around the shops first of all. The shop which they tried first had nothing at all to suit them and they complained to the shop assistant that there was nothing to their satisfaction there. They found a shop selling all sorts of things up a small rise off the High Street and found quite a number of low-priced items there. Mary would have bought some very attractive shoes, but only one of a pair could be found.

Wenglish:

Though Mary said she 'ad nothin' decent to wear, she said she would go on the outin' with 'er Auntie Annie. It was all done at the very last minute, like, and they rose theyer tickets straight off. When they got there, they thought they'd go round the shops, first go off. The first place went into 'ad nothin' to suit them and they told the woman behind the counter straight that there was nothin' worth seein' anywhere there. They found a sort of shop-popeth up a bit of a trip off the main street an' they 'ad a tidy few bargains there. Mary was after shoes and would 'ave taken a *gorgeous* pair - but they couldn't find the butty to the one she tried on!

The Story of Red Riding Hood

Told by a mother to her little one, in the same manner as her mother, in turn, used to tell it to her.

The little dwt was wanged out and getting crotchety. "Come over by 'ere and cwtch up, and I'll tell you a story," said her mam. "Eisht now, and I'll tell you all about Red Ridin' 'ood in exactly the same way as *my* mam used to tell it to me."

Once upon a time, there was a little bit of a girl called Red Ridin' 'ood. She was only a little dwt, like you, and she lived with 'er mam and dad over by the forestry. 'Er dad worked days reg'lar in the forestry cuttin' trees down, and 'er mamgu lived a tidy step further on, on the other side of the forestry, like.

One day, 'er mammy asked Red Ridin' 'ood to take some goods to 'er mamgu who 'ad been bard-in-bed and under the doctor frages. 'She'll be glad to 'ave these things in, 'cos she 'aven't been able to get about, poor dab. You'll go won't you?'

'A course I will,' said Red Ridin' 'ood.

'You better shape yourself then,' said 'er mam, ' 'cos it's a tidy step back and fore, and keep youer eyes open for that wicked wolf who do live over by there in the forestry!'

Red Ridin' 'ood thought she better put on 'er red cloak an 'ood 'cos it might come on to rain nasty, and then, off she went, full fuss to 'er mamgu's…

Now, that wicked wolf 'ad gone over mamgu's, dragged 'er out of bed, shoved 'er out of the way, cwtched, so no one could see 'er, and 'e jumped into bed to take mamgu's place …

When Red Ridin' 'ood got to mamgu's, she was out of puff with rushin' up the trip. She put the goods in the back kitchen and went into the middle room to see 'ow mamgu was getting' on.

She said, 'There' big eyes you got, mamgu'.

'That's so I cun see you tidy,' said the wolf.

'There' big ears you got,' said Red Ridin' 'ood.

'Theyer so as I cun *'ear* you tidy', said the wolf.

'Jew, there's big your mouth is!' said Red Ridin' 'ood.

'That's by there for me to gobble you all up!' said the wicked wolf, an' 'e took 'olt of 'er cloak to ketch 'er!

Red Ridin' 'ood was flabbergasted – it shook 'er rigid – but she was kokum. She shiggled 'er way out of that cloak an' was out of there like a winky. She went off, full pelt, along the road to where 'er father was 'ard at it. Talkin' twenty to the dozen she told 'im all that 'ad 'appened. 'E took 'is chopper, ran all the way back to mamgu's and gave that wolf a real belter!

'E and Red Ridin' 'ood got mamgu out of the cwtch under the stairs where the wolf 'ad put 'er. Mamgu was in 'er oils to be rescued, safe an' sound … an' they all lived 'appy ever after.

•   •   •

Mr. Rogers was talking at some length about his nearest neighbour.

"You remember", he said, "that although he's been foolish and unreliable, and we've had many serious quarrels, this time, he's been very ill. His wife has had a good deal of trouble and a bad time nursing him, poor thing. Many times, there have been almighty rows because he's been impertinent, but I do have sympathy for him now. He's getting better now and there are definite signs of improvement. The neighbours have collected for him and we've given him some fine black grapes."

Wenglish

Mr. Rogers was goin' on a bit about 'is next-door-neighbour.

"You gorrw remember", 'e said, "that though 'e've been a bit of a flag and there's no depends on 'im, an' we've quarreled 'ammer and tongs 'eaps of times, like, 'e've been real bard. 'Is wife 'ave 'ad quite a time of it with 'im an' she've 'ad a 'eavy 'and with 'im, poor dab! There've been ructions umpteen times because 'e've been cheeky beyond, but this time, like, I feel sorry (in) my 'eart for 'im. The neighbours 'ave clubbed together and we've got 'im some of them black grapes - and, by damn, theyer brammers!"

•   •   •

36

The Boy Who Cried 'Wolf'.

There was this boy, see, who atto look after the sheep for the village where 'e was livin', an 'e'd 'ad a real bellyful of it and wanted to down tools.

"You want youer 'ead read, you do!" said 'is father when the boy grizzled to 'im about it, "that's you all over, that is! For shame on you! – do you good it will, up by there on the mountin' in the fresh air doin' a tidy job, days reg'lar … a real lambastin' is what youer askin' for, for shuer, if you don't alter youer stroke sharpish!"

So the boy atto knuckle down an' carry on seein' to them sheep. To make things a bit livelier for 'im, one day 'e shouted at the top of 'is voice, "Wolf! Wolf!". When the people of the village came out with sticks and mandrels to 'elp 'im, an' clodges to aim at the wolf, there was no wolf to be 'ad, a course ...

The boy was landed now, an' in 'is oils, an' 'e thought it was graate to flummox the others, so 'e tried it on a few days later, an' agen, out they all came, full pelt, to 'elp 'im shoo off the wolf. But once agen, when they got there – no wolf to be 'ad!

This went on frages till they was all proper fed up with 'im an' 'is tricks an' they was all real moithered, like.

Now, one day, a wolf really *did* come out a the forestry to 'ave a go at them sheep. But when the boy shouted for all 'e was worth for 'em all to come an' give 'im a 'and, nobody budged an inch, an' that wolf 'ad a real beanfeast!

The boy was sorry in 'is 'eart now, a course, an' 'e could see what a flag 'e'd been. There was a lot of palaver about it, an' the boy didn't know where to put 'imself from then on …

The moral of this story is: "Don't you ever tell fibs, will you? 'Cos if you do, nobody will believe a word you do say – even when youer tellin' the trewth tidy!"

John Edwards undertook many after-dinner engagements illustrating the art of speaking Wenglish.

'Wenglish' CDs featuring John Edwards with live audiences are also available:

'Wenglish Revised'

'The Best of Wenglish' Volume 1

'The Best of Wenglish' Volume 2

'Wenglish Stories'

All are available from:

Black Mountain Records
1 Squire Court
The Marina
Swansea SA1 3XB

Telephone 01792 301500

Publisher's footnote: Tidy people everywhere should agree and fervently hope that John Edward's timeless little classics shall *never again* disappear from the shelves!